BOB DYLAN

By Geoffrey M. Horn

WORLD ALMANAC® LIBRARY

Please visit our web site at: www.worldalmanaclibrary.com
For a free color catalog describing World Almanac® Library's list
of high-quality books and multimedia programs, call 1-800-848-2928 (USA)
or 1-800-387-3178 (Canada). World Almanac® Library's fax: (414) 332-3567.

Library of Congress Cataloging-in-Publication Data

Horn, Geoffrey M.
    Bob Dylan / by Geoffrey M. Horn.
       p. cm. — (Trailblazers of the modern world)
    Includes bibliographical references and index.
    Summary: Profiles Bob Dylan, a singer and songwriter for over forty years who is known
for such songs as "Blowin' in the Wind," "Just like a Woman," and "Things Have Changed,"
the Academy Award winning song from the film, "Wonder Boys."
    ISBN 0-8368-5076-9 (lib. bdg.)
    ISBN 0-8368-5236-2 (softcover)
    1. Dylan, Bob, 1941-—Juvenile literature. 2. Rock musicians—United States—Biography—
Juvenile literature. [1. Dylan, Bob, 1941-. 2. Musicians. 3. Rock music.] I. Title. II. Series.
ML3930.D97H67   2002
782.42164'092—dc21
[B]   2002024167

This edition first published in 2002 by
World Almanac® Library
330 West Olive Street, Suite 100
Milwaukee, WI 53212 USA

This edition © 2002 by World Almanac® Library.

Project editor: Mark J. Sachner
Design and page production: Scott M. Krall
Photo research: Diane Laska-Swanke
Editor: Betsy Rasmussen
Indexer: Walter Kronenberg
Production direction: Susan Ashley

Printed in the United States of America

1 2 3 4 5 6 7 8 9 06 05 04 03 02

TABLE of CONTENTS

Words that appear in the glossary are printed in **boldface**
type the first time they occur in the text.

CHAPTER 1

ROCK'S GREATEST POET

For more than forty years, Bob Dylan has been writing, performing, and recording his own songs. When he arrived in New York's Greenwich Village at the beginning of 1961, he was a college dropout, a baby-faced nineteen-year-old strumming his guitar on street corners and singing in coffee houses for a few dollars a day. Today, he is one of the world's most admired and most imitated **singer-songwriters**. He has been inducted into the Rock and Roll Hall of Fame and the Songwriters Hall of Fame and honored by cultural and political leaders of the United States at the Kennedy Center in Washington, D.C.

Many of the folk musicians he knew and played with in the early 1960s have long since left the music scene: some have died; others have faded away. Almost alone among the creators and performers of that era, Dylan still makes news when he makes music. His forty-second **album**, *Time Out of Mind* (1997), topped many ten-best lists and won a Grammy award as Album of the Year. Critics were just as enthusiastic about his forty-third album, *Love and Theft* (2001), which received a rare five-star write-up in *Rolling Stone* magazine.

Bob Dylan was a young rebel when he performed at the Bitter End in New York City in 1961.

So what is it about Dylan? He certainly did not become a Hall of Famer on the strength of his guitar, harmonica, or keyboard playing. As for Dylan's voice, critic Dave Marsh called it "nasal and nasty, raw as barbed wire"—and he meant that as a compliment!

One way to describe Dylan's achievement is that he proved you did not have to be a great musical instrument player or have a beautiful voice, as long as you performed with energy, passion, and conviction—and if you had something to say. And yes, Dylan, the greatest rock poet ever, always had something to say. The quality of Dylan's writing in songs like "Mr. Tambourine Man," "My Back Pages," "It's All Over Now, Baby Blue," "Like a Rolling Stone," "Visions of Johanna," and "Sad-Eyed Lady of the Lowlands" set new standards for pop music.

When Dylan began recording, few people thought a pop song could be great poetry. While he was growing up in Minnesota, the song that turned him on to the thrill of rock and roll was Little Richard's "Tutti Frutti," which was recorded in 1955. "Tutti Frutti" is a firecracker of a record, but no one seems likely to nominate its explosive opening line—"Awopbopaloobopalopbamboom!"—for a poetry prize any time soon. The same thing could be said about early Beatles hits like "Love Me Do" and "She Loves You." Much of what the mature Beatles knew about writing song lyrics, they learned from listening to Bob Dylan.

Of course, what Dylan had to say was not always what audiences wanted to hear. When Dylan put down his folk guitar and started playing full-tilt rock and roll

At a black-tie gala in 1997, Dylan was honored for lifetime achievement by the Kennedy Center in Washington, D.C.

in the mid-1960s, loyal folk music fans were outraged. When he veered away from rock and started crooning country songs at the end of the decade, hard-core rock fans lost interest. And when he became a **born-again Christian** in the late 1970s and started singing Christian songs and preaching from the stage, many of his longtime fans were not too happy about that, either.

BREAKING THE RULES

Dylan has made a career out of breaking the rules and doing the opposite of what people expected. Along the way, he radically changed people's ideas of what a pop song could be. Let's consider a few music business "rules" that Dylan broke.

Radio stations will not play anything longer than three minutes. "Like a Rolling Stone," which rose to number two on the U.S. pop chart in 1965, ran more than six minutes, an unheard-of length for a pop **single**. Paul McCartney, who first listened to the record at John Lennon's house in England, later said, "It seemed to go on and on forever. It was just beautiful. . . . He showed all of us that it was possible to go a little further." The success of "Like a Rolling Stone" opened the way for other "too long for radio" hits, including the Beatles' "Hey Jude" and that all-time FM favorite, Led Zeppelin's "Stairway to Heaven."

We write 'em, you sing 'em. Many hits in the early rock and roll era were not written by the singers or groups who recorded them. Instead, professional song-writers who worked in offices in New York City,

Springsteen on Dylan

Once hailed as the "new Dylan," Bruce Springsteen was chosen to speak on January 20, 1988, when Bob Dylan was inducted into the Rock and Roll Hall of Fame. Here is part of what Springsteen said that night:

Dylan was a revolutionary. Bob freed your mind the way Elvis [Presley] freed your body. He showed us that just because the music was innately physical did not mean it was anti-intellectual. He had the vision and the talent to make a pop song that contained the whole world. He invented a new way a pop singer could sound, broke through the limitations of what a recording artist could achieve, and changed the face of rock and roll forever. . . . To this day, wherever great rock music is being made, there is the shadow of Bob Dylan. . . . So I'm just here tonight to say thanks, to say that I wouldn't be here without you, to say that there isn't a soul in this room who does not owe you his thanks.

Bruce Springsteen was called the "new Dylan" when he began recording in the early 1970s. Shown here at a concert in 1999, Bruce—or "the Boss," as fans now call him—is a major artist in his own right.

Nashville, or other big cities were expected to churn out the songs. The record company or the **producer** then decided which artists would perform them. Dylan's success as a singer of his own songs in the 1960s proved, once and for all, that the person best equipped to record a song is often the person who wrote it. This is the important idea on which singer-songwriters as different as Joni Mitchell, Stevie Wonder, Bruce Springsteen, Elvis Costello, and Ani DiFranco have based their careers.

The Byrds had a huge pop hit in 1965 with their folk-rock version of "Mr. Tambourine Man."

Dylan loved the way Jimi Hendrix recorded "All Along the Watchtower" in 1968.

Stick to the style you know best. Many recording artists have a consistent style. The record company and the audience know what to expect, and the artist is careful not to disappoint them. Dylan showed that he could explore many styles—folk, rock, pop, blues, country, gospel, even reggae and rap—and still make music that is unmistakably Dylan. Other artists who have followed this more difficult path include Ray Charles, Willie Nelson, and Lucinda Williams.

Play your hits and make them recognizable. Even today, most touring bands try to play their music the same way they recorded it. Audiences at concerts expect to hear the hits the way they sound on their boom boxes, car stereos, and home CD players. Dylan, on the other hand, has always wanted to make his music sound as loose-jointed as possible. That did not always make his listeners happy, and it could prove maddening for the musicians who played alongside him. "He used to come on one night and play real fast," one **sideman** complained. "Then next night he'd play the same songs real slow. . . . He never played anything the same way twice."

This approach had its pitfalls. On an off night, the music could sound muddled, garbled, out of control. But Dylan's strategy for keeping things fresh helped him continue to make groundbreaking music at age sixty and beyond.

A Dylan Dozen

These twelve songs mark major milestones in Dylan's career and in the history of popular music.

1. "Blowin' in the Wind" (1962). Made popular by Peter, Paul and Mary in 1963 and adopted by the civil rights movement.
2. "Percy's Song" (1964). An underground classic.
3. "The Times They Are a-Changin'" (1963). Folk protest anthem.
4. "Mr. Tambourine Man" (1964). A number-one hit and a folk-rock landmark when **covered** a year later by the Byrds.
5. "Subterranean Homesick Blues" (1965). Dylan's view of the United States during the Vietnam War.
6. "Like a Rolling Stone" (1965). Critics rank Dylan's recording as one of the great singles in rock and roll history.
7. "Rainy Day Women # 12 & 35" (1966). Known for its raucous chorus, "Everybody must get stoned."
8. "All Along the Watchtower" (1968). Most often heard in the electrifying Jimi Hendrix version recorded in 1968.
9. "Lay, Lady, Lay" (1969). Country-style Dylan at his most tuneful.
10. "Hurricane" (1975). Champions the cause of boxer Rubin "Hurricane" Carter.
11. "Gotta Serve Somebody" (1979). Dylan as a born-again Christian.
12. "Things Have Changed" (1999). An Oscar winner as Best Song for the film *Wonder Boys*.

Of the four Beatles, George Harrison had the closest friendship with Dylan. The two performed together in New York's Madison Square Garden at a 1971 benefit concert for Bangladesh.

CHAPTER 2

HIBBING DAYS

Bob Dylan was born on the night of May 24, 1941, at Saint Mary's Hospital in Duluth, Minnesota. He was not known as Dylan then. His name at birth was Robert Allen Zimmerman, the son of Beatrice (Beatty) and Abraham Zimmerman. His younger brother, David Zimmerman, was born five years later.

Early in his career, when he came to New York City, Dylan made up fantastic stories about himself. He had Sioux Indian blood, he might say. He came from the Dust Bowl region of Oklahoma. He was an orphan, raised in New Mexico. He had run away from home and joined a carnival in his early teens. None of this was true, but it gave the shy, insecure, and inexperienced young man an air of mystery and excitement.

Dylan was known as Bobby Zimmerman while growing up in this house in Hibbing, Minnesota.

MIDDLE-CLASS BOYHOOD

The simple and much less exciting truth was that Dylan grew up in a close-knit, middle-class, Jewish household. His parents were married in 1934 and lived in Duluth, on the shores of Lake Superior, until 1947, when they moved northwest to the iron-mining town of Hibbing. The reason for the move was not a happy one. In 1946, soon after Beatty gave birth to David, Abraham was stricken with polio. Decades later, Dylan recalled the toll the disabling disease had taken on his family: "My father never walked right again and suffered much pain his whole life. I never understood this until much later, but it must have been hard for him because before then he'd been a very active and physical type guy."

The Zimmermans had relatives in Hibbing. Abraham went into business with his two brothers managing an electrical appliance store, and Beatty took a job as a department store clerk. In 1948, the family moved to a two-story house at 2425 7th Avenue East. The two brothers shared one of the three upstairs bedrooms; the basement was turned into a pine-paneled recreation room. The Zimmermans were among the first families in town to get a television set, in 1952.

Two years later, in keeping with Jewish tradition, Bobby Zimmerman had his **bar mitzvah** when he turned thirteen. The reception was a gala event, with four hundred guests at the Androy Hotel, not far from where the Zimmermans had their store. At school, Bobby was sometimes teased about his Jewishness. Some classmates called him "Zennerman" or "Zimbo," or perhaps worse. Probably this was one reason why, more and more, Bobby thought of himself as an outsider.

During his short film career, James Dean expressed the anger and frustration that Dylan also felt.

REBELS AND IDOLS

For Bobby Zimmerman, as for millions of other restless teens growing up in mainstream America in the mid-1950s, movies and music showed a way to a wider world. His first movie favorite was James Dean, who gave a smoldering performance as a troubled teen in *Rebel Without a Cause*. Bobby was fourteen the year the film came

Two of Dylan's musical heroes were country star Hank Williams (above) and rock and roll singer Buddy Holly (below). Like Dean, both died young.

out. He went to see it at least four times. He cut out pictures of Dean from magazines and displayed them in his bedroom, and he was one of the first kids in town to buy a red leather jacket like the one the actor wore on screen. Dean's brief but brilliant career ended on September 30, 1955, when the twenty-four-year-old film star was killed in a high-speed car crash in California. When Dean died, "Bobby's whole world crashed in," his brother said.

Another of Dylan's early idols, country singer Hank Williams, likewise met an untimely end. Williams had an openly emotional singing style and a gift for grafting honest, heartfelt lyrics onto traditional-sounding tunes. He was also a deeply troubled young man, pained by a bad back for most of his life, dependent on painkillers and alcohol. He passed out in the backseat of his car while on tour at the age of twenty-nine and was pronounced dead in West Virginia on January 1, 1953.

A third Dylan idol also died young. On January 31, 1959, while a senior in high school, Bobby traveled from Hibbing to Duluth to hear a concert by one of rock's first great singer-songwriters, Buddy Holly. Three days later, at age twenty-two, Buddy Holly was killed in a plane crash in Iowa. "Bobby just went into mourning," his brother recalled.

"I was born with death around me," Dylan told a reporter for *Life* magazine in 1964. "I was raised in a town that was dying."

FROM ZIMMERMAN TO DYLAN

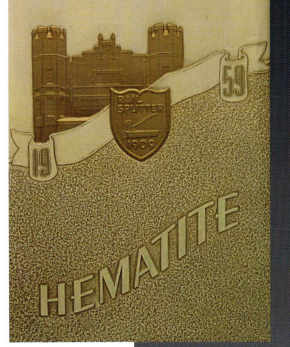

Bobby's first instrument was the piano, which—in the spirit of Little Richard—he played hard and loud. One classmate remembers a high school talent show in 1957 at which Bobby screamed out a Little Richard tune while pounding the keyboard in a style that was way too wild for most Hibbing tastes. (According to legend, he stomped so hard he broke a pedal during the performance.)

His first band, the Shadow Blasters, did not last very long, but a second group, the Golden Chords, began to pick up a local following. "We were just the loudest band around," Dylan said later. After his parents bought him a used Harley Davidson motorcycle, he made frequent trips to Duluth, where he practiced guitar with a cousin and a friend. Soon he was doing lead guitar and vocals with a Duluth-based band, the Satin Tones, imitating Buddy Holly and Elvis Presley whenever anyone would listen. With another band, the Rock Boppers, which he formed in 1958, he started using a stage name, Elston Gunn. The first name sounded like Elvis; the last name likely came from Peter Gunn, a TV detective show.

Bobby Zimmerman was a rock and roller in high school. "Hematite," the Hibbing High School yearbook, reported that his ambition was "to join 'Little Richard.'"

"WE'LL REMEMBER ALWAYS..."

Robert Zimmerman: to join "Little Richard"—
Latin Club 2; Social Studies Club 4.

Shirley Zubich: not least, but usually last—
F.N.A. 3, 4; F.B.L.A. 3, 4; Masquers 3, 4; Social Studies Club 4; Pep Club 4; Girls' League 3; Jr.-Sr. Prom Committee 3; "Stag Line" production 3.

Stephen LeDoux: to do better with each passing day—

Margaret Spinelli: forever having her seat changed—F.B.L.A. 3; Jr. Red Cross 3; Pep Club 2, 3; Girls' League 2; Jr.-Sr. Prom Committee 3.

In addition to absorbing whatever popular songs could be heard on local AM radio, Bobby and his friends would listen to the blues music they found when tuning their radios to faraway stations late at night. He also began exploring the work of modern folk musicians like Huddie Ledbetter (Leadbelly), Woody Guthrie, and Odetta. These artists did not need pumping pianos or juiced-up **amplifiers** to get their message across. All they needed was a solo guitar and the force of their powerful personalities.

In the autumn of 1959, he enrolled at the University of Minnesota, in Minneapolis. Not long after, he began performing as a **folksinger** at the Ten O'Clock Scholar, a coffee house near campus. When he returned home to Hibbing for a visit in December, the former high school student who had pounded the keys like Little Richard was now carrying an **acoustic guitar** and singing the praises of folk music.

Young Bobby Zimmerman was not performing as Elston Gunn anymore. He told his Hibbing friends he had taken a new name, Dylan—spelled D-y-l-a-n, like Dylan Thomas, the well-known modern poet. Not a bad name for a folksinger who would soon prove that he, too, had a way with words.

Don't Look Back

Dylan has not visited his hometown very often since he left Hibbing in 1959. Hibbing, a city of about seventeen-thousand people, still does not seem to know what to make of its most famous son. Plans to turn Dylan's boyhood home into a museum fell apart when the house on the corner of Seventh Avenue and 25th Street was sold to a private buyer. Downtown, Zimmy's Grill and the local public library have displays of Dylan **memorabilia**.

Who Was Dylan Thomas?

The twentieth century's other famous Dylan was born in Wales on October 27, 1914. He dropped out of school to work as a newspaper reporter at the age of sixteen and published his first book, *18 Poems*, to rave reviews when he was twenty. He was poor for much of his life, and he had a serious drinking problem. He died in New York City on November 9, 1953, at the age of thirty-nine. Thomas toured the United States several times in the early 1950s, giving readings on college campuses. Many poets who came of age in the 1950s looked to Dylan Thomas as the model of what a poet should be: wildly gifted, a risk taker with a powerful thirst for life, and, sadly, a raging talent for self-destruction.

Bob Dylan based his name on that of a well-known Welsh poet, Dylan Thomas, who died in 1953.

CHAPTER 3

MOVING ON

Dylan arrived in New York City on a snowy day in January 1961. He had already been living away from home for more than a year, hanging out (and sometimes performing) at the Ten O'Clock Scholar and other clubs, sleeping at friends' houses, and listening to every folk record he could get his hands on. During the summer of 1960, he had hitchhiked to Denver, Colorado, where he sampled the folk scene and met a young singer named Judy Collins, who would later record nearly two dozen Dylan songs. Unable to find a Denver folk club that would book him as a performer, he had returned to Minneapolis by the end of the summer.

Dylan stopped off in Hibbing in December 1960 to tell his parents he was heading for New York—and to ask his father for the money to get there. Abraham Zimmerman did not approve of the direction his son's life was taking, and he did not like the fact that Bobby had stopped using the family name. But he let his son have the money anyway, believing he had Bobby's agreement that if music did not pan out, his son would give up his dream and go back to college.

LEARNING FROM WOODY

Dylan came to New York for all the obvious reasons. Then, as now, the city was a magnet for talented young artists, musicians, and writers. Greenwich Village had a thriving folk scene, and it was still possible to find a cheap apartment in lower Manhattan.

He also had a less obvious reason for wanting to come to New York. For much of the past year, he had been studying the words and music of Woody Guthrie, an American folksinger and songwriter who spent most of his final years in the New York City area. Woody composed more than one thousand songs, some of which—"This Land Is Your Land," "So Long It's Been Good to Know You"—are still well known today. He sang and wrote about workers and drifters, farmers and ordinary folks, and he championed their cause against the wealthy and the powerful.

Dylan had begun to dress like Woody, sing like Woody, even talk like Woody, with a nasal Oklahoma twang. It was the voice, said Dylan, that first attracted him. "Hearing his voice, I could tell he was very lonesome, very alone, and very lost out in his time. That's why I dug him. Like a suicidal case or something. It was like an adolescent thing—when you need somebody to latch on to, you reach out and latch on to them."

One of the very first things Dylan did after he arrived in New York City was head out to visit Woody in the hospital. Woody was suffering from Huntington's chorea, a brain disease for which there was no

Woody Guthrie had a strong influence on Dylan and other folksingers in the 1960s. This photograph was probably taken in 1967, not long before he died.

Meeting Mimi and Joan

This is how Mimi Fariña, the sister of singer Joan Baez and a popular and well-regarded singer in her own right, recalled her first encounter with Dylan in 1961:

I met Bob Dylan one June night in 1961 at Gerde's Folk City in Greenwich Village. My parents and I were in New York because we were traveling to Paris the next day, where we were to live for two years. My sister Joan and I just had to come down to this club and see the Village to enjoy that new thing that was going on. So I did. I can almost remember what I was wearing.

We got to the club, and my first impression of Dylan was of this little guy pacing around in the back. He sang that night, but the important part for me was that I was introduced to him and others by Joan. There was a wonderful spirit in the place—lots of writers, lots of hovering, lots of discussions about songwriting. There was a real vibe and a definite uniqueness about the atmosphere of creative writers gathered together communicating to one another about their writing. . . . The Village was a wonderful scene to step into at age sixteen.

THE FOLKLORE CENTER

Presents

BOB DYLAN

IN HIS FIRST NEW YORK CONCERT

SAT. NOV. 4, 1961   8:40pm

CARNEGIE CHAPTER HALL
154 WEST 57th STREET • NEW YORK CITY

All seats $2.00

Tickets available at: The Folklore Center
                             110 MacDougal Street
GR 7 - 5987   New York City 12, New York

cure. Dylan visited him often during 1961, and through Woody, the younger man was able to meet some of the other leading lights of American folk music. Woody, who died in 1967 at the age of fifty-five, was a powerful influence not only on Dylan but also on many other folksingers in the 1960s.

FIRST BIG BREAKS

Dylan played at many folk hangouts during that first year in the Village. He performed at the Cafe Wha, Izzy Young's Folklore Center, the Gaslight, the Limelight, the Fat Black Pussycat, and the Village Gate, but most of all he was a fixture at Gerde's Folk City. By summertime, he had caught the attention of Robert Shelton, the folk music reporter for the *New York Times*. The *Times* was the most influential newspaper in town, and when Shelton wrote a glowing review of a twenty-year-old kid with uncut hair and rumpled clothes, the music business was quick to take notice. "When he works his guitar, harmonica, or piano and composes new songs faster than he can remember them, there is no doubt that he is bursting at the seams with talent," the *Times* critic raved.

By chance, the *Times* piece appeared in print on September 29, 1961—the same day Dylan was in a Columbia recording studio for the first time, playing harmonica backup for folksinger Carolyn Hester. Soon, he was topping the bill at Gerde's and had his own Columbia contract. In November, he began recording his first album, *Bob Dylan*, which was released in March 1962. The album consisted of thirteen songs; eleven of them were traditional folk songs, and two of them were Dylan originals.

The choice of the two original songs was revealing. The first was "Talking New York," done in a "talking

Dylan had been singing and playing for months at folk hangouts in Greenwich Village before he gave what was billed as his first uptown "concert" in November 1961 (facing page, top). During that first year in the Village, he met folksinger Joan Baez and her younger sister Mimi. This photo (facing page, bottom) shows Mimi (left) and Joan performing together at the Newport Folk Festival in 1968.

blues" style that Woody Guthrie had made popular. In this song, Dylan told the story of his first year in New York, poking fun at himself and at the music business. The second original was "Song to Woody," a tribute to his great friend and teacher.

Rumor has it that *Bob Dylan* was recorded in six hours, at a cost of only about $400. That is fortunate, because Dylan's debut album is believed to have sold only about five thousand copies in its first year of release.

FINDING HIS VOICE

His second album, *The Freewheelin' Bob Dylan*, met a much more enthusiastic reception. Released in May 1963, *Freewheelin'* reveals a singer who is starting to emerge from the shadow of Woody Guthrie and find his own voice. It consists mostly of original songs, ranging in tone from the angry "Masters of War" to the quieter, more personal "Don't Think Twice, It's All Right."

Two songs on the album deserve special comment. The first is "Blowin' in the Wind," which opens *Freewheelin'*. With its hopeful words and easily singable melody, this has become one of Dylan's best-loved songs. The structure of the verses is simple: a series of questions focusing on the evils of hate, bigotry, cruelty, and war—and the way some people turn a blind eye and a deaf ear to those evils. Dylan himself did not think much of the song. ("I wrote that in ten minutes," he said.) But his **manager**, Albert Grossman, was sure that in the right hands, its anti-racist message could move millions. He gave it to Peter, Paul and Mary, a singing group he also managed. Their sweet voices and uplifting harmonies were a much better fit for AM radio at that time than Dylan's own rough singing style, and the song became a pop hit during the summer of 1963.

The second song of special importance is "A Hard Rain's A-Gonna Fall." Dylan wrote this song in October 1962, when the United States and the Soviet Union faced off over the presence of Soviet missiles in Cuba, and the world came close to nuclear war. The surface meaning of

The cover of Dylan's second album, *The Freewheelin' Bob Dylan*, shows him with Suze Rotolo, his girlfriend in the early 1960s.

The vocal group Peter, Paul and Mary had a big hit with their sweetly harmonized version of "Blowin' in the Wind."

"Blowin' in the Wind"

The complete lyrics to Dylan's most famous song.

How many roads must a man walk down
Before you call him a man?
Yes, 'n' how many seas must a white dove sail
Before she sleeps in the sand?
Yes, 'n' how many times must the cannon balls fly
Before they're forever banned?
The answer, my friend, is blowin' in the wind,
The answer is blowin' in the wind.

How many times must a man look up
Before he can see the sky?
Yes, 'n' how many ears must one man have
Before he can hear people cry?
Yes, 'n' how many deaths will it take till he knows
That too many people have died?
The answer, my friend, is blowin' in the wind,
The answer is blowin' in the wind.

How many years can a mountain exist
Before it's washed to the sea?
Yes, 'n' how many years can some people exist
Before they're allowed to be free?
Yes, 'n' how many times can a man turn his head,
Pretending he just doesn't see?
The answer, my friend, is blowin' in the wind,
The answer is blowin' in the wind.

"hard rain" is nuclear fallout, the deadly poisons that would fall from the sky after an atomic blast. But "hard rain" also stands for something much bigger: the end of life as we have come to know it.

He took the tune from a traditional folk melody, but the words are rich, dense, dark, and full, like a passage from the Bible. "Every line in it is actually the start of a whole song," he said. "But when I wrote it, I thought I wouldn't have enough time alive to write all those songs so I put all I could into this one."

How Many Times?

If recordings by other singers are any guide, "Blowin' in the Wind" is the most popular song Dylan has ever written. Other performers have covered it more than 360 times, according to **"Dylanologist"** Olof Björner, a Swede who runs a fan site on the World Wide Web. Foreign language versions include German ("Die Antwort weisst ganz allein der Wind"), Swedish ("Och vinden ger svar"), French ("Dans le souffle du vent"), Hungarian ("Mit fúj a szél"), and Catalan ("Escolta-ho en el vent"). In second place is "Don't Think Twice, It's All Right," with more than two hundred cover versions.

Dylan sang "Blowin' in the Wind" and "A Hard Rain's A-Gonna Fall" at the Bangladesh benefit concert organized by George Harrison in 1971.

CHAPTER 4

CHANGING TIMES

The 1960s were a period of enormous change in American life. Some of the most important changes were taking place in the South, where African Americans had been deprived of their most basic civil rights. Led by the Reverend Martin Luther King Jr. among others, the **civil rights movement** worked to improve conditions for African Americans and to make the nation a freer and fairer place to live. Dylan wrote songs about the victims of injustice, and he sang "Blowin' in the Wind" at one of the most important civil rights rallies, the March on Washington in August 1963.

Another way the country was changing was in how people viewed U.S. relations with other countries. For decades, the United States and the Soviet Union had been locked in a **cold war**. Each nation saw the other as a threat, and each country built huge armies and stockpiled large numbers of nuclear weapons to deal with that threat. Songs like Dylan's "Masters of War" and "A Hard Rain's A-Gonna Fall" questioned where all this would lead.

Along with the cold war, the United States was becoming more deeply involved in a shooting war in Vietnam. Some Americans supported the **Vietnam War** as a way to keep the people of Southeast Asia from losing their free-

Dylan helped the civil rights movement by performing at the March on Washington in August 1963.

dom. Others thought there was no good reason for U.S. soldiers to be in Vietnam in support of what they felt was a corrupt South Vietnamese government. Dylan did not actively protest the Vietnam War, but his songs raised doubts about whether war was a good way to solve American, Vietnamese, or anyone else's problems.

Hairstyles, clothing styles, musical styles, views about drugs and sex—these, too, were changing. Millions of young Americans welcomed these changes. Many of their parents did not. Perhaps the twenty-two-year-old Dylan was thinking of his own father when he wrote these lines in "The Times They Are A-Changin'," the title song to his February 1964 album:

> "Come mothers and fathers
> Throughout the land
> And don't criticize
> What you can't understand
> Your sons and your daughters
> Are beyond your command
> Your old road is
> Rapidly agin'.
> Please get out of the new one
> If you can't lend your hand
> For the times they are a-changin'."

Copyright © 1963; renewed 1991 Special Rider Music

The high point of the 1963 March on Washington was the "I Have a Dream" speech by Martin Luther King Jr.

Demonstrators protesting the Vietnam War faced off against military police at the Pentagon in Washington, D.C., in 1967.

ANOTHER SIDE OF BOB DYLAN

The 1960s also brought major changes in Dylan's personal life. The year he landed in New York City, he took up with Suze

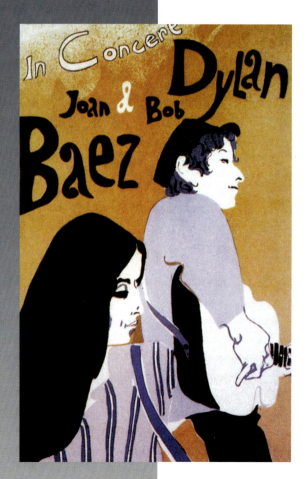

This concert poster was designed by Eric von Schmidt, a painter and folk-blues guitarist and singer who knew both Dylan and Baez well.

Rotolo, a seventeen-year-old who, when she first met Dylan, was living in the Village with her mother and her sister Carla. He credited Suze, who was a talented artist, with introducing him to the works of the great French poets. The connection with Carla was helpful, too. She had a job working for Alan Lomax, who was an expert on American folklore. Through Carla and Lomax, Dylan had access to a treasure trove of folk music on records. The relationship with Suze ended badly, with an angry argument between Dylan and Carla in early 1964.

By the time he broke up with Suze, Dylan was already involved in an affair with Joan Baez, regarded as the reigning queen of folk music in the early 1960s. Baez had a beautiful singing voice, which Dylan did not. She also had a large and devoted following, which Dylan lacked when the two first became lovers in 1963. What she saw in him was a supremely gifted poet whom she wanted to shelter and protect. The two became frequent companions, both on and off the road. For extended periods, they lived together at her house in Carmel Highlands, California. Living nearby were Joan's sister, Mimi Fariña, and her husband, Richard. Dylan had first met Richard in 1961, when Richard—like Dylan, a writer and folksinger who loved motorcycles—had been married to Carolyn Hester.

Dylan's relationship with Baez soured in the spring of 1965. He was already cheating on her with Sara Lowndes, a former model who was working in New York for Time-Life Films. Joan met Sara for the first time in May 1965, while Baez was giving a concert in London, England. Dylan, who had refused to allow Joan to join him on his own tour of England, had promised to attend her performance at Albert Hall. He sent word, however, that he could not come because he was in the hospital with a bad stomach. She went to visit him at the hospital—and there at the door to his hospital room was Sara. "All in all," said Baez, "the whole thing was the most demoralizing experience in my life. I have never understood how he could suddenly change, as if everything he had done before had never really happened."

Dylan and Sara were married on November 22, 1965, while she was pregnant with their first child, Jesse. In all, they had four children together (he also adopted a daughter she had in a previous marriage) before divorcing in 1977.

ELECTRIFYING!

What happened to Dylan in the mid-1960s was difficult for some people to watch. After the March on Washington, he made no more appearances at political rallies. He turned his back on the folk music scene. He

The romance between Baez and Dylan paired the reigning queen and king of American folk music.

Dylan secretly married Sara Lowndes in 1965, four years before this photo was taken.

A Second Marriage

Although Dylan tried to keep his wedding to Sara Lowndes secret from his friends, his family, and the world at large, the marriage eventually became public knowledge. It took much longer for the public to learn that Dylan was secretly married a second time—to one of his backup singers, Carolyn Dennis. In his book *Down the Highway: The Life of Bob Dylan* (2001), a British writer, Howard Sounes, revealed that Bob and Carolyn married in June 1986, after she gave birth to their daughter, Desiree Gabrielle Dennis-Dylan. According to Sounes, the couple divorced in October 1992. The divorce settlements with Sara and Carolyn cost the singer-songwriter millions of dollars.

Many other women have also said that Dylan was their lover. One of them, Ruth Tyrangiel, sued him for $5 million in 1994, claiming that she had lived with him from 1974 to 1993 and had even helped him write some of his songs. The case was settled out of court.

drifted away from some old friends and quarreled with others. He abused his body with drugs.

All that is true. Yet, the other important truth about Dylan in the mid-1960s is that he was writing and recording some of his most brilliant music. As he turned more and more from a folksinger into a rock star, his lyrics became ever more dazzling and his music far more urgent. As a teenager, he had wanted to be Little Richard; later he had wanted to be Woody Guthrie. In the three great albums he released in 1965 and 1966, he managed to fuse the best of both worlds.

The first album to emerge, in March 1965, was *Bringing It All Back Home*. The opening cut, "Subterranean Homesick Blues," sets a torrent of short, rhyming phrases on top of a driving rock rhythm. It is sung in Dylan's most insistent voice, and it is a barbed attack on mainstream American values and politics during the Vietnam War era. At least three other songs— "Maggie's Farm," "Gates of Eden," and "It's All Over Now, Baby Blue"—have also become classics. But the song that had the most enduring influence is "Mr. Tambourine Man," which sets some of Dylan's most dreamlike poetry to one of his most beautiful tunes. Covered by the Byrds, who had a number one pop hit with it in the summer of 1965, the song remains a folk-rock landmark.

The single that followed "Mr. Tambourine Man" to the top of the charts was the Rolling Stones' "(I Can't Get No) Satisfaction." It was still riding high when Columbia issued "Like a Rolling Stone," the first single from Dylan's second 1965 album, *Highway 61 Revisited*. This song—the one that broke AM radio's three-minute barrier—was basically an extended put-down of a "princess" who has fallen from privilege and becomes a homeless drifter. The song title, with its nod to the British rock group, was also a signal that Dylan was now playing in the big leagues of rock and roll stardom.

Highway 61 Revisited, Dylan's second album of 1965, featured the hit single "Like a Rolling Stone."

BOB DYLAN HIGHWAY 61 REVISITED

CHEERED, BOOED, AND "STONED"

Not everyone was impressed. In late July, Dylan brought his electrified act to the Newport Folk Festival in Newport, Rhode Island. The music was loud, the sound system

"Like a Rolling Stone"

Here are the opening lines of Dylan's biggest hit single, a landmark in the history of rock and roll.

Once upon a time you dressed so fine
You threw the bums a dime in your prime, didn't you?
People'd call, say, "Beware doll, you're bound to fall"
You thought they were all kiddin' you
You used to laugh about
Everybody that was hangin' out
Now you don't talk so loud
Now you don't seem so proud
About having to be scrounging for your next meal.

How does it feel
How does it feel
To be without a home
Like a complete unknown
Like a rolling stone?

was poor, and some folk fans were outraged. Dylan was booed off the stage. Whatever the reaction among folk diehards, Dylan saw no reason to change course. *Bringing It All Back Home* had cracked the top ten in album sales, and *Highway 61 Revisited* was an even bigger seller.

In May 1966, Dylan released his third album in fourteen months. *Blonde on Blonde* now fits snugly on a single CD, but when originally issued, it was a double album, its fourteen songs spread across the four sides of two long-playing records. The album contained some of his most tender lyrics, including "Just Like a Woman" and the haunting "Visions of Johanna." It also included

"Sad-Eyed Lady of the Lowlands," which, at over eleven minutes, took up the whole of side four. Dylan later revealed that the song was written as a gift to his wife. Only a little bit of imagination is needed to hear her name—Sara Lowndes—in the "Sad-Eyed Lady of the Lowlands" title and chorus.

The album's most successful and controversial single was the romping, stomping "Rainy Day Women #12 & 35." This song was Dylan's answer to critics of all kinds. Whoever you are, whatever you do, "they'll stone ya," he repeated again and again. The chorus ("Everybody must get stoned") was both a statement of fact (anyone can be a target of unfair criticism) and, many listeners thought, an open endorsement of drug use. The events of the next few months would give the singer the chance to rethink his views.

Dylan tried to look tough on the cover of *Blonde on Blonde,* but the double album offered some of his most tenderly beautiful songs.

CHAPTER 5

NEW DIRECTIONS

Sometime around sunup on July 29, 1966, while staying at Woodstock, New York, Dylan went out for a spin on his beloved Triumph motorcycle. No one is sure exactly what happened that morning. The singer has said, at various times, that he hit an oil slick or was blinded by the sunlight. What does seem clear is that he panicked and hit the brake too hard, causing his back wheel to lock up, and he lost control of his cycle.

Rumors flew that Dylan was dead, that he was the target of a murder plot, that his face was cut so badly he would no longer appear in public. None of this, of course, was true. He spent a week or more in the hospital before returning to Woodstock to rest. He had hurt his back, and visitors to Woodstock reported that he was wearing a neck brace. His injuries, however, were not life threatening—although they did lead Dylan to do some hard thinking about his life and music.

For a year and a half, the pressures on him had been mounting. He had released three albums—three of the most important albums in the history of American music. He had toured the United States, Europe, and Australia. More concerts were planned, and he was under contract for a novel, a TV show, and yet another album. He was worn down— by travel, by drugs, by the stress of trying to top what he had already accomplished. When he had the accident, he said later, "I woke up and caught my senses. I realized I was just workin' for all those leeches. And I didn't want to do that. Plus, I had a family."

This 1968 photo on the cover of a national magazine heralded the growing influence of country music on Dylan's style

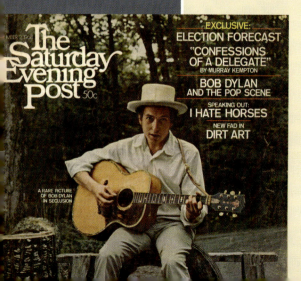

For the remainder of 1966 and most of the following year, Dylan stayed in Woodstock, spending time with his wife and growing family. (Sara gave birth to a daughter, Anna, in the summer of 1967.) During this period, he also worked with a group of musicians who had settled in the nearby town of West Saugerties

Richard, Mimi, Joan, and Bob

Three months before Dylan's accident, Richard Fariña was killed in a motorcycle crash in California. The date was April 30, 1966, and Fariña had just left a book-signing party for his newly published novel, *Been Down So Long It Looks Like Up to Me.* It was also Mimi Fariña's twenty-first birthday.

Mimi, who had recorded two folk albums with her husband, continued to live and make music on the West Coast after his death. In 1974, she founded an organization called Bread & Roses, which offers free concerts for the elderly and other shut-ins living in the San Francisco Bay area. Mimi died of lung cancer on July 18, 2001.

Joan Baez has continued to record and perform. She toured with Dylan in the mid-1970s as part of the Rolling Thunder Revue. Of Joan's own songs, the most successful is "Diamonds and Rust" (1975), which describes her relationship with Bob.

and lived in a brightly painted house they named Big Pink. The group, including Robbie Robertson on **electric guitar**, had toured with Dylan during the crazy years of the mid-1960s. As Dylan's backup band, they were known as the Hawks, but when their first album, *Music from Big Pink*, appeared in 1968, they called themselves simply the Band.

For most listeners, the first inkling of the changes in Dylan's life and music came with the release of *John Wesley Harding* in late December 1967. This album, which was recorded in Nashville, Tennessee (the capital of country music), was completely different from anything the Beatles or the Rolling Stones were doing. *John Wesley Harding* consisted of twelve songs that were mostly short, lean, and stark. Instead of electronic gimmicks and studio wizardry, the album spotlighted the

Dylan often performed with a group known first as the Hawks and then as the Band, which included guitarist Robbie Robertson (right).

Like their cover art, the Beatles' recordings became more and more elaborate in the mid-1960s.

The simple cover and spare sound of *John Wesley Harding* were in stark contrast to what the top British pop groups were doing.

spare sound of Dylan's own voice and harmonica, supported by bass, drums, and, on the last two cuts, the pure country twang of a steel guitar. Even the album art was a surprise. In contrast to the bright colors and costumes of the Beatles' *Sgt. Pepper's Lonely Hearts Club Band*, which topped the album charts for much of the year, the *John Wesley Harding* cover art was muted, and the photo of Dylan was in black and white.

"Tears of Rage," "This Wheel's on Fire," and "I Shall Be Released," three Dylan songs performed by the Band on

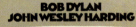

Big Pink, had a fuller, richer sound—something of a combination of country, blues, gospel, and rock. Meanwhile, the Byrds, who had a 1965 folk-rock hit with "Mr. Tambourine Man," developed their own brand of country-rock with a catchy Dylan tune, "You Ain't Goin' Nowhere."

Other songs that Dylan and the Band played into a tape recorder in the basement of Big Pink came out in a **bootleg** recording with crummy sound that appeared in 1969 and was snapped up by eager fans. An official version, *The Basement Tapes*, did not become available until six years later.

FOLLOWING NEW PATHWAYS

Many people who had cheered the rock-and-roll Dylan were shocked by his laid-back country style on *Nashville Skyline* (1969). They were also startled by the lyrics, which substituted pop country's traditional singsong rhymes for the wildly poetic language of his earlier work. Looked at now, the move to country seems less surprising. Young Bobby Zimmerman had been an avid country music listener. He had idolized Hank Williams before he ever heard Little Richard or met Woody Guthrie. In the mid-1960s, he had become friends with a Nashville legend, Johnny Cash, who championed his music. Cash joined him on *Nashville Skyline* for a duet on "Girl of the North Country." Another album cut, the lovely "Lay, Lady, Lay," proved to be one of Dylan's most popular singles.

Dylan's music in the 1970s met with an uneven reception. One reason was his changing style, which confused some listeners. (Was he folk? Was he rock? Was he country? Was he rhythm and blues?) Another reason was that he just was not composing as many good songs as he had earlier. Two albums in mid-decade enjoyed excellent reviews and robust sales: *Blood on the Tracks* (1975), written during the breakup of his marriage with Sara, and *Desire* (1976), spurred by the playing of Scarlet Rivera, a fiddler he met in Greenwich Village. Other recordings had a few good cuts mixed with too many that were forgettable or sloppy or both.

Reviewers were not very kind to his works in other media either, including

Many rock fans were turned off by the country sound of *Nashville Skyline*.

Desire begins with "Hurricane," one of Dylan's most effective protest songs.

his long-delayed novel *Tarantula* (1971). Critics were likewise unimpressed with Dylan's acting in a 1973 western, *Pat Garrett and Billy the Kid*, for which he also wrote the music. And they were brutal in dismissing *Renaldo and Clara* (1978), a film Dylan loosely based on his Rolling Thunder Revue tour of the mid-1970s. "It all looks pretty silly," said one critic of the movie, in which Sara, Joan Baez, and poet Allen Ginsberg also appeared. The film, which in its original version ran nearly four hours, received a somewhat warmer greeting in Europe.

Dylan played a character named Alias in the film *Pat Garrett and Billy the Kid*.

Joan Baez joined Dylan onstage for a 1975 "Night of the Hurricane" concert at Madison Square Garden in New York City. Both singers had their faces painted white, which was part of Dylan's performing style while touring in the Rolling Thunder Revue.

"Hurricane"

The first song on *Desire* marks a return to the kind of protest ballad that had first made Dylan famous. "Hurricane," which he co-wrote with Jacques Levy, tells the story of a middleweight boxer, Rubin "Hurricane" Carter. Carter's ring career ended when he was convicted, along with another black man, of killing three whites in a barroom shooting in 1966. Dylan believed Carter was innocent and wrote "Hurricane" to help clear his name. Carter was freed in 1985, when a judge ruled that the guilty verdict had been based on "racism rather than reason." *The Hurricane* (1999), a film about the case, starred Denzel Washington and featured Dylan's song.

BORN AGAIN

Dylan spent most of 1978 on an extended tour of Japan, Australia, Europe, and the United States. In November, while in Tucson, Arizona, the desperately worn-out and road-weary singer had a vision. "There was a presence in the room that couldn't have been anybody but Jesus. . . . Jesus put his hand on me. It was a physical thing. I felt it. I felt it all over me. I felt my whole body tremble. The glory of the Lord knocked me down and picked me up." Five days later, concertgoers in Fort Worth, Texas, noticed that the son of Abraham Zimmerman was wearing a metal cross around his neck.

When *Slow Train Coming* was released in August 1979, the Christian message was there for all to hear. Many reviewers praised the music on the new album, which had a soul-gospel flavor. But some concert audiences did not take kindly to Dylan's preaching from the stage. He wanted to spread the Word. They wanted to hear the hits.

Although Dylan had become a born-again Christian by 1983, when this photo was taken, he donned traditional Jewish prayer garments while attending his son's bar mitzvah in Jerusalem.

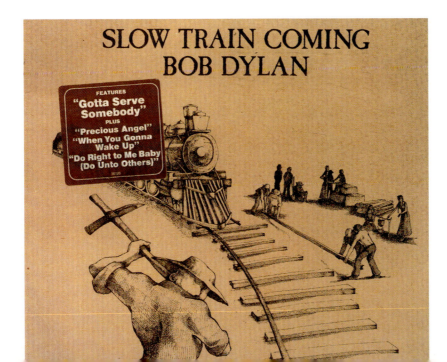

The Christian message of *Slow Train Coming* heartened some listeners and troubled others.

CHAPTER 6

THE NEVER ENDING TOUR

Bob Dylan celebrated his fortieth birthday in May 1981. He had already outlived the heroes of his youth—Hank Williams, James Dean, and Buddy Holly. He had also outlived some of the brightest lights of the rock and roll era, including Jimi Hendrix, Elvis Presley, and John Lennon.

His career in the 1980s and early 1990s seemed to echo these lines from "Tangled Up in Blue":

"And when finally the bottom fell out
I became withdrawn,
The only thing I knew how to do
Was to keep on keepin' on like a bird that flew,
Tangled up in blue."
Copyright © 1974 Ram's Horn Music

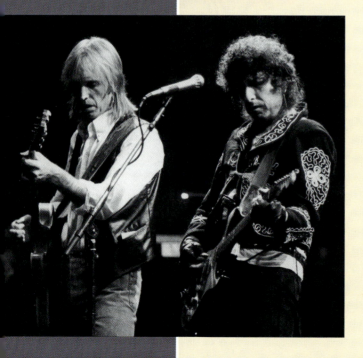

Tom Petty (left) and Dylan toured together in the mid-1980s. Later they performed as the Traveling Wilburys, along with George Harrison, Roy Orbison, and Jeff Lynne.

ON THE ROAD

"Keep on keepin' on"—that is what Dylan did, through performance after performance, even as critics carped and album sales slowed. He launched major tours in 1981 and 1984, then returned to the road with Tom Petty and the Heartbreakers in 1986 and the Grateful Dead in 1987. He released several albums of new material, mostly to lukewarm reviews, and even appeared on a rap record.

Dylan went on the road with the Grateful Dead in 1987. Fronting the band along with Dylan were Dead members Bob Weir (left) and Jerry Garcia (right).

One of Dylan's more successful projects of the 1980s was *Biograph* (1985). Far more than a standard "greatest hits" package, *Biograph* contained over four dozen tracks, including some rare, previously unreleased items. It also boasted excellent liner notes by Cameron Crowe, a rock writer who has since become an extremely successful filmmaker. This multidisc album set the pattern for many boxed-set tributes to other artists.

Near the end of the decade, Dylan recorded an easygoing effort with four other musical heavyweights: Tom Petty, Roy Orbison, Jeff Lynne, and former Beatle George Harrison. The aging rockers, who called themselves the Traveling Wilburys, reunited for a second album—but without Orbison, who died of a heart attack in December 1988, soon after the first album appeared.

By then, Dylan had launched what he called the Never Ending Tour. The choice of continents and cities changed. The clubs and concert halls changed. The musicians changed. The songs changed. Even the way Dylan sang the songs changed. What did not change was the fact that night after night, year after year, he was out on the road. "I found out I could do it effortlessly," he told *Rolling Stone* magazine in 2001. "I could sing night after night and never get tired."

Biograph went far beyond the standard "greatest hits" formula to give Dylan fans a deeper understanding of his life and career.

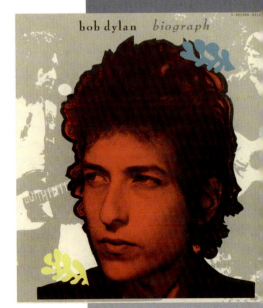

The Rapper

Rap music pioneer Kurtis Blow first met Dylan in 1983, when the two men were working in nearby rooms at the Power Station recording studio in New York City. Dylan asked if he could use some of Blow's backup singers, and the rapper said yes. Dylan returned the favor by agreeing to rap on one of Blow's albums. Here is how Blow described the experience of working with Dylan:

We played him the song, and I told him what part I wanted him to do. He went right into the studio by himself, learned the lyrics, and knocked it out in one take. I was shocked and amazed. I've written raps for . . . all kinds of entertainers that don't really rap. I write the raps, they go home and practice, and then come back to try it. It usually takes them several hours to get it done. This guy wrote the rap down, went into the studio, and knocked it out in one perfect take. I was thinking, "Bob, you don't even have to think about doing that one again—it's great." I was floored. It was like, okay, that's it. Time to go home. We were there maybe half an hour. He's a great guy. So cool. He's to himself a lot, quiet, doesn't talk that much. But when he does, his voice is very humble and calm.

A LIFETIME IN MUSIC

As he approached his fiftieth birthday, Dylan could point to a growing list of honors he had received. He was admitted to the Songwriters Hall of Fame in March 1982 and to the Rock and Roll Hall of Fame in January 1988. Two years later, he received France's highest cultural award, the Commander of the Order of Arts and Letters. In 1991, the National Academy of Recording Arts and Sciences—which had managed to overlook all of Dylan's landmark albums in the 1960s—belatedly voted him a special Grammy Lifetime Achievement Award.

To honor the thirtieth anniversary of Dylan's first studio recording, Columbia staged a "Bobfest" at New York's Madison Square Garden in October 1992. The performers, chosen to represent five decades of rock history, included Johnny Cash, Willie Nelson, Stevie Wonder, George Harrison, Eric Clapton, Neil Young (singing "All Along the Watchtower"), Tom Petty and the

Film actor Jack Nicholson (right) presented Dylan with a Grammy Lifetime Achievement Award in 1991.

Heartbreakers (singing "Rainy Day Women #12 and 35"), Mary Chapin Carpenter, Tracy Chapman, Chrissie Hynde of the Pretenders, Eddie Vedder of Pearl Jam, and, of course, Bob himself.

A CAREER REVIVED

In January 1997, Dylan went into the recording studio to make his forty-second album, *Time Out of Mind*. To oversee the sessions, he chose Daniel Lanois, who had produced *Oh Mercy* (1989), one of Dylan's better-reviewed efforts of the 1980s. Lanois, a French Canadian, gave *Time Out of Mind* a mood somewhere between twilight and midnight—dark, bluesy, swampy, and mysterious. On "Cold Irons Bound" and other tracks, Dylan's voice, worn from years of hard traveling, growled as much as sang.

In May, while Columbia was waiting to release the new album, Dylan was admitted to a Los Angeles hospital with a heart infection. The condition was serious, and the singer was forced to cancel his summer tour. "I'm just glad to be feeling better," he said. "I really thought I'd be seeing Elvis soon."

His brush with death, coupled with the grim power of the new album, brought Dylan his best press coverage in many years. In September, he was invited to perform in Bologna, Italy, at a concert arranged by the Vatican. He was greeted warmly by Pope John Paul II, who in a speech earlier that day

Fans have learned to expect the unexpected at Dylan performances. A prankster with the words "Soy Bomb" spray-painted on his chest had to be hustled offstage at the Grammy Awards show in 1998.

Paul Simon (right) was Dylan's touring partner in 1999.

had quoted from "Blowin' in the Wind." In December, in the presence of President Bill Clinton and other U.S. leaders, Dylan was honored in Washington, D.C., at the Kennedy Center for the Performing Arts.

The following February, Grammy voters capped off Dylan's remarkable thirteen months by choosing *Time Out of Mind* as Album of the Year. Dylan also won awards for Best Contemporary Folk Album and Best Male Rock Vocal Performance (for "Cold Irons Bound"). In addition, he had the satisfaction of seeing Jakob Dylan, his youngest son by Sara, win two Grammy awards as leader of the Wallflowers.

Bob Dylan's sixtieth birthday in 2001 brought new honors and another powerhouse album. In March, he won his first Academy Award, an Oscar for Original Song for "Things Have Changed," from the film *Wonder Boys*. The new album, *Love and Theft*, was released in September. Lighter in mood than *Time Out of Mind*, it won reviews even more glowing than the earlier work. Rock, blues, country, pop—Dylan put a new twist on just about every American song style. "It says much for the seemingly limitless renewability of Bob

Dylan's creative gifts that *Love and Theft*, his forty-third album, should sound as distinctive and intriguing in 2001 as his debut did nearly forty years earlier," raved a British reviewer, Andy Gill.

BOB DYLAN

"Love And Theft"

Leading critics called *Love and Theft* the best album of 2001.

This concert in Norway in 2001 was one of many hundreds of stops on the Never Ending Tour.

"NO FLASH IN THE PAN"

Love and Theft earned Dylan another Grammy for Best Contemporary Folk Album. On Grammy night, in February 2002, he gave a knockout performance of "Cry A While." The song is raw and powerful, with lyrics that are sometimes funny, sometimes angry. The message is complicated, but one line rings out loud and clear: "I don't carry dead weight—I'm no flash in the pan."

Each year, rock sees a new crop of one-hit wonders. In his seventh decade of life, Dylan is an aging figure in a business that is built on hot young talent. But rock's greatest poet is not about to give up. Amazingly, after dozens of albums and thousands of live performances, Dylan is still making music that people want—and need—to hear.

TIMELINE

1941	Robert Allen Zimmerman is born May 24, in Duluth, Minnesota
1947	Moves from Duluth to Hibbing, Minnesota
1959	Makes his debut as a folksinger; calls himself Bob Dylan
1961	Arrives in New York City; begins performing there; meets Woody Guthrie
1962	First album, *Bob Dylan*, is released; sales are disappointing
1963	*Freewheelin' Bob Dylan* is released; performs at the March on Washington
1964	*The Times They Are A-Changin'* and *Another Side of Bob Dylan* are issued
1965	*Bringing It All Back Home* and *Highway 61 Revisited* are released; Byrds top the charts with "Mr. Tambourine Man"; Dylan has a hit single with "Like a Rolling Stone"; secretly marries Sara Lowndes (they divorce in 1977)
1966	*Blonde on Blonde* appears; injured in a motorcycle accident
1967	*John Wesley Harding* is released
1968	First concert appearance in twenty months, at a Woody Guthrie memorial
1969	*Nashville Skyline* reveals his new country music style
1971	*Tarantula* is published
1975	*Blood on the Tracks* is issued; the Rolling Thunder Revue is launched
1976	*Desire* is issued
1979	*Slow Train Coming* release confirms that Dylan is a born-again Christian
1986	Secretly marries his backup singer Carolyn Dennis (they divorce in 1992)
1988	Inducted into the Rock and Roll Hall of Fame; Never Ending Tour is launched
1990	Named Commander of the Order of Arts and Letters
1991	Receives a Grammy Lifetime Achievement Award
1997	Survives a serious heart infection; greeted by Pope John Paul II; honored for lifetime achievement at the Kennedy Center in Washington, D.C.
1998	*Time Out of Mind*, released in 1997, is the Grammy Album of the Year
2002	*Rolling Stone* critics pick Dylan as 2001 Artist of the Year and *Love and Theft* as top album

GLOSSARY

acoustic guitar: a guitar that is not plugged into an amplifier

album: a collection of songs issued together on one or more long-playing phonograph records, audiocassettes, or compact discs

amplifiers: electrical devices that change the sound of guitars or other musical instruments and make them louder

bar mitzvah: ceremony that takes place when a Jewish boy becomes thirteen, marking his entry into adulthood

bootleg: an album or other media recorded or sold illegally

born-again Christian: someone who develops an intense personal faith in Jesus

civil rights movement: protests and demonstrations in the 1950s and 1960s aimed at winning freedom and equality for African Americans in the United States

cold war: a long period (1945–1990) of superpower rivalry between the United States and the Soviet Union

covered: a performed or recorded song that was first performed or recorded by someone else.

Dylanologist: someone who has made a career out of studying Dylan's life and music

electric guitar: a guitar that is played through an amplifier

folksinger: a person who sings traditional songs (or modern songs composed in a similar style)

manager: someone who takes care of a musician's business affairs

memorabilia: a collection of items connected with a famous person or event

producer: the person in charge of a recording session, who is responsible for the overall sound of the recording

sideman: a musician who supports the leader in a band

singer-songwriters: singers who write nearly all the songs they perform and record

single: a short recording of an individual song, often paired with a song of lesser importance

Vietnam War: a war fought by the United States in Southeast Asia from the late 1950s through the mid-1970s

TO FIND OUT MORE

BOOKS

Curtin, John and Bob Dylan. *Bob Dylan Made Easy for Guitar.* New York: Music Sales Corp., 1994.

Dylan, Bob. *The Definitive Dylan Songbook.* New York: Omnibus Press, 2001.

Heylin, Clinton. *Bob Dylan: A Life in Stolen Moments: Day by Day, 1941–1995.* New York: Music Sales Corp., 2000.

Johnson, Tracy (ed.). *Encounters with Bob Dylan: If You See Him, Say Hello.* Daly City, Calif.: Humble Press, 2000.

INTERNET SITES

About Bob Dylan
www.bjorner.com
Listings of recording sessions, concert appearances, and key dates in Dylan's life.

Bob Dylan
bobdylan.com/
The official site with lyrics and brief sound clips for hundreds of Dylan songs.

Bread & Roses
www.breadandroses.org/
Organization founded by Mimi Fariña.

Country Music Hall of Fame
www.halloffame.org/
Explore Dylan's country roots through biographies of Hank Williams and others.

Rock and Roll Hall of Fame
www.rockhall.com/
Short biographies of many of rock and roll's greatest stars.

Woody Guthrie Foundation and Archives
www.woodyguthrie.org/
The life and legacy of the great American folksinger.

INDEX (continued)

About the Author

Geoffrey M. Horn is a freelance writer and editor with a lifelong interest in politics and the arts. He is the author of books for young people and adults, and has contributed hundreds of articles to encyclopedias and other reference books, including *The World Almanac*. He graduated summa cum laude with a bachelor's degree in English literature from Columbia University, in New York City, and holds a master's degree with honors from St. John's College, Cambridge, England. He lives in southwestern Virginia, in the foothills of the Blue Ridge Mountains, with his wife, five cats, and one rambunctious collie. This book is dedicated to Michael Dylan Horn.